m

D1427029

Cooking a Home

A collection of the recipes and
stories of Syrian refugees

Pilar Puig Cortada

authorHOUSE®

AuthorHouse™ UK
1663 Liberty Drive
Bloomington, IN 47403 USA
www.authorhouse.co.uk
Phone: 0800.197.4150

Published by AuthorHouse 02/10/2015

ISBN: 978-1-5049-3669-9 (sc)
ISBN: 978-1-5049-3670-5 (e)

Print information available on the last page.

Any people depicted in stock imagery provided by Thinkstock are models, and such images are being used for illustrative purposes only. Certain stock imagery © Thinkstock.

This book is printed on acid-free paper.

Contents

This book would have not been possible without the participation and encouragement of so many. It is dedicated to all those that it made it possible, starting by the Syrian refugees that were generous enough to share their story with me. I would also like to thank my friends, who kindly edited these pages. To all of you: thank you.

Fast Forward
to a Peaceful Delicious Syria

By Afra Jalabi

I was asked to write this forward on a short notice, but like any Syrian woman, I thought I could cook up something quickly. As I started to write, I became filled with a longing to create a recipe to literally fast-forward to a peaceful, free, and democratic Syria.

Yes, we need a recipe to rescue Syria. After all, everything we do is really a recipe in which different ingredients are put together, with specific tools and processes, heated with energy and power and voila, you've got a great meal!

Pilar has written the kind of cookbook that I sometimes dreamt of writing— collecting the stories of the recipes in my family—of my late mother, aunts and grandmothers on both sides of the family as well as those of my friends. There are always, in every family, enticing stories about particular meals, and after hearing them you want to get up, pull up your sleeves and recreate the meal and ambiance. I was never into books with collections of mechanical recipes. We don't just eat when we sit at a table. We tell stories and the food in front of us is telling us many stories.

Seeing so much of Syria go up in flames we want to grab what we can and hide it in the aprons of our memories and the pantries of our identity. My family, whose homes were destroyed under shelling, lost most of the family photos, including the ancient ones in sepia and black and white. Those that were scanned and copied are now so cherished. My aunt's rose garden is in ruins and sometimes I wonder if some of the bushes are blooming without any care despite the shelling and bombing. My uncle who is a writer lost many of his notes in his Golan home, some were retrieved by friends and some shrivelled and dissolved under the rain falling through the open roof.

But the recipes survive. They sneak through borders and are smuggled in the despairing hearts of the migrating ones. When I visit my relatives in Istanbul we cook together; our old recipes of Mahashi (stuffed vegetables) and some new Turkish ones my relatives are picking up and my usual heretical combinations of all that I inherited and learned along my own perpetual migration from Syria. This is the power of really good cooking. Once you're steeped in a good gourmet tradition you can create new interpretations and adapt into local ingredients and customs. But this is also the real battle on all fronts: The struggle between tradition on the one hand and reform and innovation on the other. I have relatives who raise their eyebrows when they see me put Quinoa instead of Bulgur (cracked wheat) in Tabouleh. And my mother in law taught me to grate one clove of garlic into the well-established roasted vermicelli rice recipe. She would say, "It makes it more fragrant, but don't tell anyone." Over dinner when people would sing praises about the amazing rice recipe she'd wink at me. This is why the stories Pilar tells make you want to recreate the food. Because it is written in a way where you are invited into the lives of people who suffered but who were once w allowed to eat comfortably but not allowed to think or speak comfortably. In fact, in many ways, Syrians—despite the repression or maybe because of it—excelled in some of their culinary inclinations. If Syrians couldn't talk about much and were not allowed to be creative in anything that impacted public life then they could really excel in food. And so like most people on the planet we think we make the best food. I'm sure you heard this everywhere, but in our case we have serious evidence. The joke among some Syrians is that we got too busy perfecting our recipes and carving out zucchinis and rolling vine-leaves that colonial powers came and colonized us in our gastronomical delirium, and then before we got awakened our local armies took over again.

However, I also know that those who excel in the kitchen can cook up some serious storms. Syrians initiated a peaceful revolution and were patient for several months. But with the constant brutality a beautiful country got caught in the prison of greed and power. And so in the land of the best food and culinary genius everything has been going up in flames. Moreover the regime used food as a weapon by starving some areas under siege. In response, some friends, Syrian and American, launched together early in 2014 a hunger strike in solidarity with Syrians. Many of us participated and later also regained a different meaning of fasting when Ramadan arrived in the summer. Some Syrians still fast a day or two a week in spiritual solidarity with Syrians. If food is political so is fasting. And in between these extremes we become far more sensitised about a world which swings between people dying of hunger and others dying of gluttony.

Our challenge as Syrians, but also as fellow inhabitants on this planet is to turn our world into a large kitchen, in which we feed the needy, resolve conflict around tables with words and coffee —and not with grenades and bombs—and fill our pantries with tools and nourishment that would raise our youth—and not with chemical weapons and poison gas. If we acted like good cooks and good parents we'd be more concerned about the physical and mental wellbeing of our growing generations and we'd put some of our best energies into making this world a gentler place for all of us.

Cooking is not a simple matter. Trust me on this. It is a great political tool even at the smallest level, particularly at the personal level. Learn some of these recipes and see how your social life could suddenly shift. Don't be shocked if you start becoming popular among your friends, and like I do when I can't convince people of my political views and especially about the power of nonviolence, I "hit" them with a good meal. They are much more likely to listen after stuffed chicken and green-peas rice. And here is a cheating-out for stuffed vegetables. If you are revolutionary and want to save people and the environment and want to save trees and stop torture around the world you won't always have the time to sit and carve out the zucchinis; just get some colourful bell peppers and use the same recipe for stuffing. It will still look impressive, minus a great deal of preparation time.

The recipes in this book are seriously delicious. They are basic and simple but also sophisticated. Invite your friends, cook them a Syrian dinner and discuss ways of supporting Syria in concrete ways like the real food you're eating. My ultimate wish though is that you get the chance to visit a peaceful Syria in the near future and find out for yourself how the perfection of our food has finally caught up with us. If we start doing politics and human rights the way we do food I fully trust the consequences.

Introduction

When I was sixteen, there was nothing I hated more than our punctual, structured, family dinners. Everyone had a defined seat at the table: my mother in front of my father, my brother next to my mother and in front of me, so that, to complete the circle, I sat next to my father. The plates, the napkins, the cutlery, the glasses… were always organized in the same manner. We couldn't just eat leftovers out of Tupperware, god forbid, but had to put said leftovers on clean plates and set them on the table. Especially bothersome to me was the fact that every single night, at 9 pm sharp, we had to try to make conversation with each other.

So I picked at my food with my fork and replied in monosyllables to my parents' annoying questions, staring down at my plate, vaguely aware that I was being unfair to them. I longed for the moment in which I would live on my own and be able to eat whatever I wanted, wherever I pleased—if it was on the floor, on the floor—and however I wished —if it was picking the food out of the Tupperware with my hands and licking my fingers immediately after, well, so be it!

All this changed when I moved away two years later. Ever since, whenever I travel or feel far from home, it is those family meals that I miss the most. I catch myself longing for the lazy weekend hours spent in the kitchen, watching my mother move around in her apron, cutting, frying, baking and washing, her hands always soft, moist and clean, and smelling of food. I miss the buzz of the extractor, how it notifies the entire family that a meal is being prepared downstairs and that it will soon be time to gather around the table to eat. I miss the fumes that emanate from the kitchen and invade the house, the smell of frying garlic and onion, of my mother's bubbling tomato stir-fry, of fresh thyme—picked from our miniscule herb garden— which decorates the chicken roasting in the oven. I remember the colour of the local tomatoes, their bright red, juicy flesh always dotted with pale green and yellow.

Even more, I miss sitting with my brother, my mother and my father at the table, in our designated places, and taking our time to eat. I miss sharing a meal with them, and with the occasional guest, while making easy, comfy, cosy conversation.

The best cure, I have come to find, is eating a big meal with friends: one that is as tasty and, more importantly, as physically and spiritually satisfying, as the ones we make back home.

As it turns out, home, for me, is a heart-warming, mouth-watering, steaming *tortilla de patata*, a cool glass of *gazpacho* or a salty, crunchy piece of *pan con tomate* topped with strips of dark, gleaming *jamón serrano*. It is the Jamie Oliver tofu curry and the famous family zucchini cake that my friends so eagerly devoured whenever they came over.

To be fair, it is not only the food that is so soothing, but also the rituals that surround it. Home is the weekend excursions my mother and I always undertake to the local markets, or to the supermarket instead, when we are in a hurry. It is the time spent in the kitchen, chopping, mixing, and smelling. It is setting the table before a meal, and cleaning up after. It is our eternal *sobremesas*—which is what the Spanish call the period after finishing a meal during which you continue to sit at the table and chat—and which we accompany with a cup of bitter coffee.

Forget the living room, the kitchen is the most important room of the house! It is the origin, the place where it all begins to bubble.

Eating, apparently, is much more than the satisfaction of a biological need; it is imbued with multiple layers of meaning. Anthropologists have long studied eating as a social phenomenon, in which markers such as social class or nationality... are enacted and reflected. It shapes and shows who we are. Caviar is a pretentious delicacy reserved for the rich and is associated to high social classes while burgers feed the masses. Paella has become a synonym for Spanish, and sushi is quintessentially Japanese.

Perhaps food takes on all these meanings because people seem to have a natural tendency to socially gather around food. A meal brings us closer, human to human. It is no wonder that so many events are structured, at least to some extent, around the act of eating: weddings, birthdays, Christmas, Iftar, art exhibition openings, business lunch meetings... We love to get together and dig in. Food helps us empathize with each other.

In 2010, UNESCO, the United Nations Educational, Scientific and Cultural Organization—which basically defines at an international level what is considered cultural heritage and what is not—, inscribed both the Gastronomic meal of the French and Traditional Mexican Cuisine on the Representative List of the Intangible Cultural Heritage of Humanity, recognizing culinary practices as significant examples of immaterial culture for the first time. In 2013, the traditional dietary cultures of the Japanese, or *Washoku*, were also added to the list.

These traditions may not be feats of architecture, like the pyramids of Giza or the Great Wall of China; they may not be evidently monumental, but they reflect a culture, the history of a people just as much. And they infiltrate and decorate our daily life with their aromas, colours and savours, tickling our taste buds with stories from the past, prickling our minds with dreams for the future, helping us grasp who we are and where we come from, all the while filling our tummies. What heritage could be more important than that which makes you feel you?

In July 2014, I had the opportunity to accompany a group of friends working on a documentary theatre piece based on the stories of Syrian refugees. Together, we travelled to Jordan, which currently hosts more than six hundred thousand registered Syrian refugees, and met with a diverse range of people.

We talked to everyone: Jordanians, NGO workers, non-refugee Syrians, Syrian refugees living in the capital, Syrian refugees living in refugee camps, well-to-do, intellectual, illiterate, and underprivileged Syrians... and found, instead of the fragile, depoliticized, victimized refugee, so often portrayed by the media, incredibly strong, welcoming, positive and creative people who struggled, and managed, to create their home in exile day by day.

I know how homesick I can get when I am far from home, and I could not even begin to imagine how you might feel after having had to flee your country, driven away by violence, destruction and the continuous threat of insecurity, without knowing whether you will ever be able to go back. I wondered if, maybe, just maybe, those meals that helped me so much might also provide comfort to those who find themselves in such extreme situations of displacement. That idea is what brought me to talk about food.

During the interviews and conversations we had in Jordan, I tried to find out more about the role cooking and eating might play in moments like those, of extended humanitarian crisis. I also asked the people we met, who had been forced to abandon their Syrian homes, for recipes that brought them comfort or reminded them of Syria.

With those recipes, I decided, I would compile some sort of book, so as to share a bit of the amazing culture I merely glimpsed at during my time with Syrians in Jordan, with others around the world. Moreover, talking about food seemed to bring the people I met some comfort and joy. It allowed for the establishment of a deep human connection and offered the opportunity for laughter and enjoyment, even when just having discussed war and death, which they still felt very near. Through my questions, I aimed to determine whether, as I suspected, food could indeed soften, even if only minimally, the harshness and painfulness of the situation.

Eating, cooking, could provide consolation to Syrians in exile and also help those living far away from the conflict and its consequences to understand and sympathize with the population affected by the Syrian civil war, I thought. It was, therefore, something worth exploring.

Many of those we talked to and interviewed, asked us to share their story with our respective countries when we got back, partly indignant at international inactivity and the world's passivity during the horrible events taking place, partly hopful that maybe, by telling about their personal plight, they could appeal to others' empathy and finally provoke a massive response from the people of the globe, one that could pressure politicians into action. It is for them, and because I share their outrage, that I decided to undertake this project.

In the following pages you will find the recipes that were given to me, accompanied by the stories of their authors and how I had the fortune of meeting them. Some recipes I learned from people who invited me into their homes, into their kitchens, and took the time to teach me how to make their chosen dish. Others were scribbled down in the notebook I took with me everywhere, in Arabic, in Spanish, in English… hurriedly annotated in the waiting room of a clinic set up for refugees, or while bidding goodbye at the end of an interview. In these cases, though I have done my best to provide complete and accurate recipes, certain steps or ingredients may have been lost.

However, that doesn't really matter because, ultimately, this book is not so much about the actual cooking or the specific recipes. It is about Syrian culture, about the social situation of refugees today, about politics, about injustice… and most of all a celebration of food as a means to enact and share our human nature.

Context

Now let me tell you a bit about the current situation.

The number of refugees that have fled Syria due to the Syrian civil war, which has already caused the death of over one hundred thousand people, amounted, in August 2014, to almost three million, over six hundred thousand of which are now residing in Jordan. Syrian refugees now represent over ten per cent of the Jordanian population.

Jordan is a small country inhabited by just fewer than eight million people and bordered by Iraq and Israel, the current wave of refugees that seek asylum, arriving from neighbouring Syria, is not the first one. Previously, Jordan received Iraqi and Palestinian refugees as well. There are over fifty five thousand Iraqi and well over two million Palestinian refugees in the country. Altogether, refugees currently make up almost a quarter of the Jordanian population.

The situation is now extremely precarious as the influx of refugees is putting an increasing strain on the Jordanian economy, which was already battling poverty, inflation, insufficient supplies of water and other resources and high rates of unemployment, which are officially set at fourteen per cent but unofficially calculated to be around thirty per cent. Many Jordanians blame refugees for stealing their jobs, they also blame them for increasing housing prices. In Northern areas like Irbid, a city near the Syrian border, where Syrian refugees represent over forty per cent of the population, tensions between locals and asylum seekers are running high.

Jordan does what it can to accommodate the new arrivals and the Syrian refugees we talked to were incredibly thankful, despite the harsh conditions they must face: they recognized the help offered by Jordan, thanking God—*alhamdullilah*—, and deeply admired the generosity the country was showing towards their people. At the same time, they admitted to sometimes feeling discriminated against by the Jordanian population and unjustly abandoned and forgotten by the rest of the world.

Though the refugee status is conceived as a basic human right, being a refugee actually involves many restrictions and hardships. For example, refugees cannot legally work in Jordan without a work permit, which is not given to Syrians at the moment, and registered refugees receive a meagre twenty-four dinars a month from the UNHCR (United Nations High Commission for Refugees). To put this in perspective: living off of twenty-four dinars a month in Jordan is somewhat like living off of twenty-four Euros a month in a European country. Jordanian taxis might be cheap in comparison to European ones, but rent is high and food is expensive. Most refugees have a very hard time making ends meet and putting food on the table. Some Syrians find illegal jobs, but the pay is low and if caught, they can face high fines, arrest or deportation.

Life is made even harder as refugees are not allowed to own property. The idea is that they are only in the country temporarily and will be leaving soon, but given the fact that a solution to the conflict seems far off still, refugees are stuck in a prolonged, uncomfortable, uncertain situation in which they find it hard to imagine, and even more to actively work towards, a future for themselves.

Difficulties do not end there. Many refugees feel their lives have been truncated. Inside the refugee camps, for example, children are able to attend classes offered by NGOs, but older students, like those who were attending higher education, have to abandon their studies: it is practically impossible to go to university while living in the camp.

Finding a job is even harder inside of the camps than it already is in the cities. One of the main complaints put forward by the refugees we interviewed in Zaatari, the biggest camp in Jordan, was the profound boredom and the horrible feeling of uselessness that emerges from not being able to earn your own bread. In these conditions, it is hard to conceive of, and even less to pursue, a future like the one that they had envisaged back home. Many refugees prefer returning to Syria, to a life of constant insecurity and fear, than to stay in Jordan. For most of those who choose to remain in exile, life is forcedly in suspension; many proclaim they are merely waiting until return to Syria is possible in order to restart their lives.

Still, even in difficult contexts like these, people share, do, live, love, eat... And they fight to make themselves a home. One of the ways to do so, I realized, is through food.

In the very beginning, in Zaatari camp, like in most refugee camps, refugees were given cooked meals that were brought into the camps by external catering services. However, after a while, refugees started to protest for they wanted to be able to make their own food. This led to the establishment of the voucher system: now refugees are given vouchers, which they can exchange for different kinds of foodstuffs, depending on their needs and likings. People in Zaatari camp can now cook their own meals, at home. Little shops have also appeared all along the camp, they offer falafels, Arabic sweets and a wide range of produce that refugees can buy. Some families have even planted their own tiny vegetable gardens, where they grow herbs with which they enrich their meals.

Being able to choose and cook your own food brings back some degree of autonomy, reassurance and normalcy. Small things like having a tiny vegetable garden can make all the difference. I was able to witness this first hand during the day we spent in Zaatari camp. Hadi and his family, whom we visited there, had planted several herbs and vegetables in a small patch of sand located within the cement grounds of their tiny, makeshift house. There, was the most wonderful smelling mint I have ever encountered, and small green, still ripening, tomatoes which looked promising. The host family was extremely proud of that little garden: it gave warmth to their home and added colour to their plates. It also provided a bit of solace: Zaatari is located in the middle of the desert; the little, bright plants reminded them of their green Syria and somewhat softened the dry, dusty atmosphere. In the camp, the dustiness is so intense that respiratory tract infection is the most common medical condition suffered by its inhabitants.

Moreover, labouring the soil to grow produce, no matter how small the parcel available, is a way of grounding oneself, the roots of the small plants pushing into the dirt almost a continuation of ones own. Those vegetable gardens were something that Syrian refugees, both inside and outside the camps, highly appreciated.

What most amazed me, though, during our meetings with Syrian refugees was the cooking. Hadi and his family, with whom we spent that morning in Zaatari camp, showed us a picture of an *Iftar* dinner they had prepared earlier that week in their home, inside the camp, and which they ate on the floor of their tiny patio: the cemented space that linked the two caravans they lived in. It was an amazing feast made up of colourful dishes, full of different concoctions, settled beautifully on the floor. In the picture, the family was gathered around, patiently awaiting the end of the day's fasting to be announced. It was a meal anyone would envy.

On a different occasion, we visited two buildings located in the outskirts of Amman, which were managed by a small NGO, most probably funded by the Muslim Brotherhood, and hosted families of disadvantaged Syrian refugees. They were modest living spaces, with small, simple kitchens. But there, we were offered homemade Syrian pastries so elegant they looked like something you would find on display in the window of a professional bakery, and they tasted just as good.

Even though Syrians are not allowed to buy property in Jordan, or be legally employed there, and have limited means combined with limitless difficulties when it comes to making a home, they sure do cook themselves one.

Recipes

Aban's *Molouhkié* and pasta with tomato "sos", the *Aleppan* way

I met Aban through Facebook. He had commented on the Facebook page of a Syrian ice cream parlour, now based in Amman, that I was investigating, saying that the new Jordanian branch brought back a lot of memories. Food and remembrance… it was exactly what I wanted to talk about. I checked out his profile: he was originally from Aleppo and now lived in Amman.

1

A week before taking off on my journey to the Jordanian capital, feeling like a true journalist, I sent him a private message telling him about my curiosity for food and the project that had ensued. I asked whether he would be willing to meet up with me to talk about Syrian cooking, about his personal experience and to maybe share a few recipes with me. Honestly, I was not expecting an answer. The situation of most Syrians now living in Jordan tends to be an extremely delicate one. A lot of them still have family back home and are afraid to talk for fear of the repercussions their loved ones might suffer in retaliation. However, Aban immediately accepted. He gave me his phone number and said to call when I was in town.

I met up with Aban the night of my arrival. It was Ramadan, people fasted during the day and Aban could only meet up after *Iftar*, the meal that breaks the fast. It was nine, we were supposed to meet at nine thirty and I was starting to feel a bit nervous. This was my first interview in Amman. I did not really know what to expect. What would we talk about and how would he react to my questions? Aban had probably been through some difficult times in the past few years and I did not want to intrude in on his personal life.

I felt very self-conscious about the fact that I was a complete foreigner, coming from a country unaffected by war, now meddling in the lives of people who had suffered and were still suffering greatly. He might not appreciate outsiders' nosiness or might mistake my honest concern for macabre curiosity.

Aban called me to say that he was on his way and to confirm whether I would be at the agreed location on time. We could barely communicate over the phone: Aban had a hard time understanding my English, which is quite American, and I had a hard time understanding his, which was very Arabic. "Great start" I thought.

The cafe was very hip. A giant blackboard covered the wall stating the drinks on offer and their prices in bright colours. I was surprised to hear Wax Taylor and Caribou playing in the background, two electronic bands that are very popular among European youth.

Aban walked smiling into the cafe. He immediately came across as a warm person, his constant smile shy but never fading. He was quite tall, much bigger than me—I am about a meter and seventy centimetres tall—, and had a lean figure. He had thick black hair and wore it combed back neatly, strictly tamed with the aid of gel. He greeted me, stiffly shook my hand and sat down, obviously feeling a bit uncomfortable. At this point, we both felt quite awkward. After asking him what he wanted to drink, I went to the counter and ordered for the both of us. I thought the minimum I could do was to pay for his drink. There were wonderful looking pies on display at the counter. I turned around and asked Aban if he wanted some food to accompany his choice of lemon juice, but he had just come from celebrating *Iftar*, finally eating after an entire day of fasting and laughed at the cultural naïveté of my question.

It was a lot easier to talk to him than I had anticipated. Aban explained that he had left Syria, along with his younger brother, back in 2012, when he was twenty-six. They had been forced to flee in order to escape attending military service. At the time, they knew no one in Jordan other than a distant relative who could not do much to help them. No friends awaited them in Amman.

Aban said he was not scared or worried about meeting with me but he asked me not to share his name—which is, of course, not Aban, the pseudonym I have given him—for if it got out, his family might suffer the consequences. His mother had not wanted him to meet up with me but he had decided to come anyways, driven by his generous hospitality. He told me he wanted to make me feel welcome, like he had not, in Jordan. I thanked him feeling the utmost respect and gratitude. It was humbling to be received so warmly.

Aban told me that he was now working as an engineer at an electronics store, after having been a salesman for a while. He made six hundred dinars a month, a very good salary for a Syrian working in Jordan. Aban felt privileged, he was obviously proud of his job and felt lucky when comparing his situation to that of other Syrian refugees. His brother worked longer days, twelve-hour shifts, with a much lower pay and was only twenty-four. They lived in a small apartment where, during Ramadan, they celebrated *Iftar* together. Aban cooked for the both of them.

"You don't celebrate with more people?" I asked. "Isn't it supposed to be a big family gathering kind of thing?" I had imagined *Iftar* to be a slightly overcrowded occasion, like Christmas family dinners.

"My brother is my family" Aban said.

I imagined the two brothers eating alone after a long day of work. It did not seem like the *Iftar* they deserved.

"Amman is expensive," said Aban. "We have no future here: if you cannot save money, you cannot have a future".

He couldn't go back to Aleppo, where his family still resided, because if he did, he would be persecuted by the regime and forced to serve in the army, or worse. Those who flee Syria are automatically labelled rebels by the Bashar government and are not welcome anymore. He couldn't travel to another country either because if he did he might not be let back into Jordan again.

"I can't do anything, I can only stay. And my family can't come, there are so many Syrians here looking for work, we can't bring in more. And I cannot pay another apartment for my family. It's better for them to stay there, even if there is war".

I asked him if he was happy. "No. How can you be happy when you don't have a future?"

When I asked Aban about food, the conversation quickly got animated. He mentioned a lot of words I had never heard before and laughed as he tried to explain basic ingredients to me, describing common vegetables.

He turned to his IPhone, "Google," he said "Google will help us!" He typed the words in Arabic in Google images and showed me the results of the searches; it was a very effective way of understanding each other. It also gave Aban the opportunity to show off his two smartphones, of which he was extremely proud. "I also have a car!" He added, "but it's illegal. So, if we drive around, we have to be careful". I thanked him but decided to turn down the offer.

That day, to break the fast, Aban explained, he had made his brother macaroni with tomato sauce. It was their favourite dish, he said, because it reminded them of Aleppo, of home. Aleppan cuisine is extremely renowned and I was utterly surprised to hear that pasta with tomato "*sos*" was what reminded Aban of his hometown. I had expected something Arabic-sounding, not mispronounced macaroni! My first day and I was already confronted with how clichéd my own conceptions were.

Aban told me his favourite Aleppan dish was, without a doubt, *Molouhkié*. Google images showed a thick green-leaf-like soup, it resembled boiled spinach.

"*Molouhkié* is made with *Chorcorus*," he explained, a green plant that looks much like the common weed. *Molouhkié* is an extremely popular dish in the Middle East: also known as the food of the people. Some say it was first eaten in Egypt, during the times of the great pharaohs. Other sources indicate that *Molouhkié* is of Jewish origin, which explains its English name: Jew's Mallow.

It is supposed to be an extremely healthy dish, full of vitamins and minerals like beta-carotene, iron and vitamin C. However, as Aban warned me several times, either you absolutely love it or you absolutely hate it. The leaves have a very bitter, particular taste and once cooked become quite mushy: both the flavour and the texture are rather surprising to those that are not accustomed to it.

There are many different ways to prepare *Molouhkié*: it can be boiled, it can be fried or it can be both boiled and fried. Sometimes chicken is added and others it is cooked with lamb. You can accompany it with rice, Arabic bread or both. However, it is almost always prepared with a combination of garlic, spices—coriander, cinnamon, and chillies— and meat. *Molouhkié* also has numerous names, and different regions pronounce it in dissimilar manners: *Mulukhiyah, mloukhiya, molokhia, molohiya, mulukhiyya, malukhiyah* or *moroheiya*, are just some of the many ways to call it according to Wikipedia.

Aban makes his *Molouhkié* the Aleppan or Levantine way: with chicken, and normally accompanies it with rice. He said it was extremely easy to make, and that he would teach me.

I asked Aban how he had learned to cook. He seemed to enjoy making food very much, which surprised me for I expected cooking to be mostly a female activity in Middle Eastern cultures. He told me he had learned by watching his mother very carefully; he said he was very observant as a child. Now that he lived on his own, he had plenty of opportunities to practice and enjoyed making the dishes he remembered being prepared back home for himself and for his brother.

The cafe was closing down. They turned off the lights signalling that it was time to leave, while simultaneously apologizing for kicking us out. We headed onto the lively streets. It was eleven and everything was buzzing: during Ramadan, most activity takes place during the night. Aban and I said goodbye and went our ways. It was exciting to be in Amman.

Though I did not get the chance to see Aban again while I was in Jordan, we are still friends on Facebook and regularly exchange a word or two and enquire about how the other is doing. He still sends me pictures of the dishes he prepares for himself and his brother and plenty of emoticons.

Aban's Allepan macaroni with tomato "sos"

Ingredients (4 servings)

1 onion
400g of ground beef
400g of elbow macaroni
200g of tomato puree
Olive oil
Salt to taste
Pepper to taste

Instructions

Chop up the onion and fry it in a large pan with olive oil, at medium heat. After a minute or two add the ground beef.

In the meantime, boil the macaroni following the times indicated by the package. When the pasta is done, add the macaroni to the pan, mix with the beef and onion, and cook over low fire. Add salt and pepper to taste.

Finally, add the tomato paste and let it cook for another minute or two and you have your macaroni with tomato sauce.

Molouhkié

Ingredients (4 servings)

400g frozen or dry *moloukhié* leaves (If you cannot find frozen or fresh *moloukhié* leaves, you can buy dry *moloukhié* leaves and soak them for two hours in cold water, then drain them and wash them instead)

4 chicken legs

Coriander

2 cloves of garlic

Olive oil

Salt

A few laurel leaves

A lemon

A cinnamon stick

Instructions

Finely chop the garlic cloves. Fry the *moloukhié* leaves in a bit of oil, over medium heat, together with half of the garlic and half a teaspoon of coriander. Make sure to stir every five minutes, until the mixture is soggy.

In the meantime, set 1 litre of water to boil in a big pot, add some lemon peel, the rest of the garlic, the stick of cinnamon and the laurel leaves, and boil the chicken until cooked. If you are boiling full chicken breasts, with skin and bones, this should take around thirty minutes. If the skin and bones have been removed then cooking time should be reduced to twenty minutes. To speed up the process, you can cut the chicken breasts into halves, and then cooking should take around fifteen minutes. When done, you should be able to cut the cooked chicken with a spoon. Add the broth from the chicken to the pan with the *moloukhié* leaves and let cook for about twenty-five to thirty minutes.

Remove the pot from the stove and serve the soup together with the chicken.

The infamous *Kousa Mahshi,* two ways

Lubna's vegetarian *Kousa Mahshi*

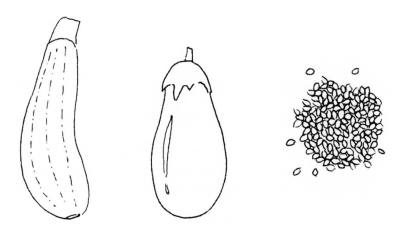

The most repeated answer to the question "What is your favorite dish?" when interviewing Syrians in Jordan, was: *"Kousa Mahshi!"*

Stuffing vegetables is a widespread culinary practice in the Middle East, it has been for centuries, and the favourite choice when it comes to filling greens with rice, spices and everything nice is zucchini, or *Kousa* in Arabic. In the Levant they use a special kind of zucchini, which is small, about half the size of your average one, and has a pale green tone. It is possible to replicate the recipe with normal zucchinis, but you might want to cut them in half—further instructions can be found at the end of this chapter. Stuffing eggplants is also quite popular, and some recipes combine both vegetables.

Especially during Ramadan its popularity increases, for *Kousa* is an all-time favourite for the *Iftar*, the meal that breaks the fast. Indeed, *Kousa Mahshi* is such a popular dish that I was given recipes for it on more than one occasion. Mind you, those I interviewed were extremely serious about their *Kousa*. There were even several discussions about what the "right" way of preparing *Kousa* was, in which interviewees gesticulated at each other while loudly arguing in Arabic. These discussions were so fervent, that I decided to include the different versions of the recipe I encountered in this book. They reflect different customs and are a witness to the diverse range of methods there are to prepare a given dish, no matter how traditional it may be. Each recipe was passionately defended as the authentic one. More importantly, though, each was equally delicious.

One of the ways to prepare *Kousa* was explained to me by Lubna. Lubna is a Syrian journalist who resided and worked for an international NGO in Amman. She had not applied for refugee status and was therefore not a registered Syrian refugee. I had contacted her via email after reading several of her articles on the life of Syrian refugees in Jordan and told her about my project. She agreed to meet.

She surprised me with her short, pixie haircut, the tips boldly dyed blond. Her look was quite audacious. She wore sunglasses and a sleeveless shirt, something I did not dare to do at any point during my stay in the Jordanian capital. I made sure to keep my shoulders covered. She was quite cool and very dry: her questions and answers always to-the-point. She talked like she was in a hurry.

Lubna did not observe Ramadan and was one of the few people who agreed to meet during the day: she wasn't fasting and was happy to join us for a cup of coffee and to exchange stories and contacts. Lubna was also the first person to tell me about *Kousa Mahshi*.

Emma (one of the friends I was working with in Jordan) and I, met with Lubna at the only cafe that opened during the day during Ramadan, the same one I had visited earlier with Aban. There, they continued to play electronic music and, this time, very loudly. It was hard to hear what she was saying over the booming drum and bass. Though Lubna assured us she had never been to the place, she ran into several people she knew while we were there. We waited patiently for her to update her multiple friends before she came back to our corner and sat down to talk with us.

Amman was very small, she said, and especially in the minute, culturally active section of the population, of which she was a part of, everyone knew everyone. You could tell immediately by how the tone of her voice changed whenever she mentioned Amman that she did not like the city much.

When I told Lubna about my interest in food and the would-be recipe book, she loved the idea. I asked her if she would be willing to share a recipe with me, to which she responded enthusiastically. Coincidentally, she told us that the day before she had been feeling very homesick and had called her mother, currently residing in Damascus with the rest of her family, to ask her how to prepare her all-time favourite dish: *Kousa Mahshi*. Lubna had not eaten it in two years, since she left Syria back in 2012. She was so proud of the result, which she referred to as a culinary masterpiece, that she had taken many pictures and posted them everywhere: Twitter, Facebook, Instagram... She took out her iPad and eagerly showed us the photographs of her marvellous, home-recalling concoction.

We asked Lubna about her background, curious to know more. She told us she was originally from Homes but had studied in Damascus, where she had also worked as a journalist. When the revolution started she felt she was in danger due to her previous journalistic activity and decided to leave the country. Her boyfriend was Jordanian, so she ended up moving to Amman with him. She didn't like life in Jordan though; she thought Jordanians were somewhat hypocritical. And, more importantly, there was absolutely nothing to do in Amman.

In the near future, Lubna hoped to study her Masters abroad, in something like media and development or social media. At the time, she was considering going to the Netherlands, but had to figure out her visas, residence permits and scholarships first. The current context made this quite tricky: if she left Jordan she might not be able to come back, so everything had to be settled and definitive beforehand, just in case she was not allowed to return. The Jordanian border was closed for Syrians.

She told us that a few weeks earlier, when coming back from a Human Rights council she had attended in Geneva, she had been detained at the airport for twelve long hours. She only managed to get back into Jordan thanks to a *Wasta*, which is the Arabic word for connections in high places: this time, a friend of her boyfriend's family was able to pull some strings, but she might not be so lucky the next time around.

Halima's meaty *Kousa Mahshi*

The recipe for Lubna's *Kousa Mahshi* is a vegetarian version of the dish, in which the zucchinis are stuffed with a mix of rice and tomato. There are, however, other ways to prepare it. Halima's *kousa*, for example, is additionally prepared with red meat, preferably lamb's meat.

We had the pleasure of meeting Halima during a visit we made to a local clinic. It was a special clinic for refugees, and our contact, Wadi, had agreed to show us around the premises and introduce us to the people working there. We visited the different departments: general medicine, a special Handicap International section, mental illness, nutrition, gynaecology, and interviewed some of the nurses and doctors that worked there. Something that really surprised me, which we were shown in the nutrition section, was the short, coloured strip they wrapped around the thin arms of children and pregnant women in order to measure and diagnose malnutrition. We were told that most of the patients came due to chronic illnesses, like diabetes. However, there were also many cases of mental illness, especially of posttraumatic stress disorder, and of war-related injuries.

After the thorough visit, we spent some time in the waiting room. There, around thirty refugees, mostly families with children, were waiting to be attended by a doctor.

Gathered around the lines of chairs filled with patiently seated people, was Halima and her family: a young teen-aged girl, two little girls of around six and seven years of age, two little boys that couldn't be older than five, and her smiling husband. The girls stayed close to Halima while her husband took care of the two carefree youngsters. Halima, who looked to be in her thirties, had an air of patience and kindness about her. We immediately felt comfortable with her.

We started by asking Halima where she came from. She only spoke Arabic, so Wadi had to translate everything for us, back and forth. But when Halima spoke, she looked us in the eyes; she did not look at the translator. Halima told us that she and her family came from a small town in Syria; they had arrived only two months earlier, and were still working on settling in. They were having a very hard time trying to make ends meet—like most of the clinic's patients they had trouble putting food on the table.

We asked her about cooking, whether they were still able to make good food. "No" she replied, and the teen-aged girl nodded in agreement. They did not have the means to buy the ingredients, nor to cook them the way they did back in Syria. Fresh produce was very expensive in Amman. You could perceive Halima's sadness when she said this, her voice, like her eyes, very soft.

We also asked her what she missed the most from back home. She didn't have to think very long before she answered that it was "al hawaha". Wadi explained what it meant: "she misses *her* air, the air of Syria, the air of the place".

When we enquired about Halima's favourite food, again the answer was quick to come: "Mahshi!" Halima replied. I asked her whether she would mind sharing her recipe for *Mahshi* with us. None of the members of Halima's family had either email or Facebook, which is quite strange, for most of the Syrians we met were extremely active on the social media, even in Zaatari camp. The only remaining option we had was to write the recipe down: there and then. I gave Wadi my pen and my notebook and he got to work, scribbling down the instructions Halima gave him in Arabic. I would worry about the translating later.

At this point, the conversation got lively. Other people sitting in the waiting room even came over to see what was happening. A man in his late seventies seemed especially curious, he got up from his chair and came closer to listen to what Halima was saying. After a while, he started gesticulating with his hands, while discussing with Halima, imitating the way you carve out and then stuff a zucchini in order to make *kousa mahshi*. His movements kept getting bigger, inflamed as they were by the enthusiasm of his words. The old man was obviously not happy with the instructions Halima was giving: "the real recipe is not like that!" Wadi informed us he was exclaiming. After about five minutes of animated exchange the recipe was successfully determined, and the discussion was resolved. They had finally managed to agree on what the "authentic" recipe consisted of.

We were surprised to realise that during the time it had taken Halima to explain how to make *Kousa Mahshi*, the atmosphere of the waiting room had changed immensely. For a moment, the tension that had been so present earlier, had disappeared. We were all laughing together: everyone cracked up when the fight about what the "proper way" to make *Kousa* was took place between the old man and Halima. The excitement was palpable. It was incredible to see that talking about food could have that effect.

Halima invited us, with the help of Wadi's translation of course, to come to her house for a meal of *Mahshi*. She even offered to teach us how to prepare it. We were overwhelmed by the kindness of her invitation, but turned it down because we did not want to bother her or her family any further, and perhaps more importantly, because Wadi had indicated – with a stern look and a shake of his head – that it would not be appropriate for us to accept. Doing so would only put a further strain on their already tight economy.

It was time to go. We got up and said our goodbyes, reluctant to end the agreeable conversation. Our words resonated with the kindness and the warmth that Halima had instilled in us. She radiated a profound beauty, a wise beauty, her gentle face elegantly framed by her hijab.

Later, when our friend Bayan, Jordanian by birth but Syrian by upbringing, translated the recipe for me, she insisted that it was all wrong: "Tsk, tsk" she went, while coolly tilting her chin up, disapproving the Arabic way. Though me and Emma tried to replicate this gesture endless times, we could never do it as convincingly as she did. Bayan, who I will further introduce later on, suggested some changes to Halima's recipe and helped me determine missing details, such as some of the cooking times, which were not annotated in the busy refugee clinic waiting room.

In the following pages you may find both Lubna's vegetarian recipe and Halima's non-vegetarian recipe, to which I have added Bayan's suggestions, for *Kousa Mahshi*.

Lubna's vegetarian *Kousa*

Ingredients

6 small-sized eggplants (or 3 normal sized eggplants), preferably already carved

6 small-sized zucchini (or 3 normal sized zucchini) preferably already carved

For the filling:

100g (½ cup) short-grain rice, washed and drained
4 tablespoons olive oil
1 tomato, finely chopped
1 onion, finely chopped
2 garlic cloves, crushed
1 lemon
4 tablespoons parsley, finely chopped
1 teaspoon of pomegranate molasses
1 teaspoon of dry mint
Salt to taste
1 lemon, sliced

For the sauce:

500ml (2 cups) of water

150g (½ cup) of dried tomato

5 cloves of garlic

1 tablespoon of salt

Cooking time: around one hour and forty-five minutes

Instructions

In Jordan, and especially during Ramadan, it is very easy to find already carved zucchini and eggplants in the local markets and supermarkets. If you cannot find already carved vegetables, then you will have to empty them out yourself. The best way to do so is by using a small, special zucchini corer called *manakra*. If you cannot find one, you can use an apple corer or a knife instead.

First, cut off the stems. If you are using normal-sized vegetables, cut them in half. Insert the *manakra* into the flesh of the vegetable and push it in, being careful to avoid puncturing it completely, making sure not to break through the other end. Turn the corer around and then pull it out again, carving out the contents. You should repeat this process until you have carved out the vegetable completely, so that it becomes a little pocket, with edges about half a centimetre wide. If you are using a knife, carefully cut out the inside of the zucchini and the eggplants.

The discarded insides of the vegetables are normally used to make little omelettes, or cooked separately and added as a side dish.

Finely chop the onion, tomato and parsley. Crush two of the garlic cloves. Then, pour all the filling ingredients into a mixing bowl and stir until thoroughly mixed. Fill the zucchini and eggplant pockets with the mixture. Keep in mind that the rice will increase in size while cooking, so make sure not to fill the vegetables to the brim. Carefully set the stuffed vegetables into a deep pot. Try to place them vertically, so that the contents do not spill out during cooking.

You can now add the sauce ingredients into the pot and set it on the stove. Bring the water to a boil and then lower the heat. Let it simmer for one hour and forty-five minutes. During the first hour you should leave the pot covered, and then uncover the pot again for the last thirty minutes.

Once the time is up, remove the *kousa* carefully, making sure not to break the, by now, extremely soft vegetables. You can eat the dish either hot or cold: both are equally delicious. *Kousa* can also be served as an appetizer.

Halima's meaty Kousa, edited by Bayan

Ingredients

Red meat (preferably lamb)
Egyptian rice (a cup per person)
Parsley to taste
Dry mint to taste
Tomato paste
One head of garlic
Black pepper to taste
Salt to taste
Zucchini
Olive oil

Instructions

Chop off the stems of the zucchinis, carefully removing them, and put them aside. They will later be used as a little cap to close the stuffed zucchinis. Carve out the inside of the zucchinis; being careful not to break the bottom of the vegetables, they have to be sturdy enough to hold the rice filling (see instructions for carving in the recipe for *Lubna's kousa*). Clean them out with water and set them aside.

Wash the rice and put it in a bowl. Mix it with two spoons of the tomato paste and the ground red meat. Fill the zucchinis with the mix and close them with the cut off stems when you are finished. Another option is to use grape leaves to close the zucchinis, stuffing them in the open end to make sure the filling does not fall out.

Put the stuffed vegetables in a pot. Add water, salt, and another two spoons of tomato paste, cover the pot and set it over high heat to cook. After a quarter of an hour, lower the heat. When the zucchinis have been cooking for around thirty minutes, add the garlic, olive oil, mint and pepper and let them cook for another fifteen minutes.

Ghalib's Galaya

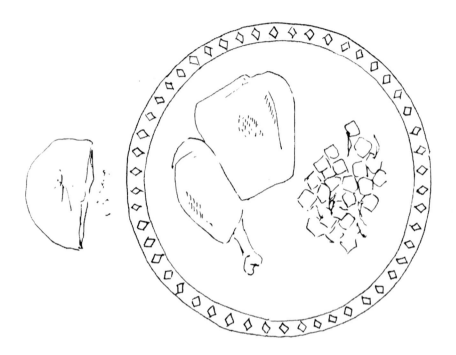

Manu was one of those people that do not fit into any categories. You just couldn't pin him down. He was in his twenties, originally from the South of Spain, and always wore gel in his hair, with which he made it stand up in little, separate spikes. He had studied Arabic literature—not the most typical career choice in Spain.

Earlier that year, Manu had received a scholarship to travel to Amman to improve his language skills. There, for six months, he studied at the local university. He had just finished the last classes of his Arabic course, and was enjoying his final weeks in the capital, hanging out with the many friends he had made during his stay, before heading off to work for Emirates airline as a steward. His plan, he told us, was to earn money while travelling the world and save up for a Masters degree, he did not know in what just yet. Manu spoke perfect Arabic.

It was Manu that put us in contact with Ghalib. He asked him whether he would be willing to be interviewed by us, and organized a meeting with him. Ghalib only spoke Arabic, so Manu translated.

We met up with Manu at his place, near the university. He was renting an apartment in a solitary building, located on the top of a hill, in what seemed to be the middle of nowhere. Ghalib worked in the same building: he was the doorman.

The taxi dropped us off on a barren hill. Luckily, Manu came out to greet us. There was no gel in his hair that day, he had just woken up he explained, excusing himself for his unkempt look. It suited him much better than his usual gelled one, I thought. He wore a wife-beater, not the most appropriate choice during the month of Ramadan, "*haram*"— naughty—, he said, and hurried us towards the lobby, not wanting to be seen in public. There was not much to worry about, though, given the fact that we were in the middle of nowhere and there was absolutely no one around.

The apartment building was big; maybe even ten stories high, and had a huge porch entrance. To the left of the porch was a table, surrounded by orange, plastic chairs and a big, fluffy, colourful couch, which was falling apart. The porch offered a bit of shade, very welcome on that bare hill. We sat around the table while Emma prepared the camera and the microphones for the interview. I strolled around, lazily eyeing the surroundings. Manu chatted with us in his usual carefree manner.

Ghalib finally came over; he was a very cheerful guy in his early twenties. He was wearing a full Adidas tracksuit, black, white and blue.

He sat down on the couch next to Manu, they hugged and laughed, obviously relaxed. Emma and I took a seat in the orange chairs across from them. We were immediately touched by how comfortable Ghalib and Manu were with each other. They were real *Habibis*.

We began the interview by asking Ghalib about his story. He was not very comfortable talking about his time in Syria, or his trip from there to Jordan and he did not want to do so while in front of the camera. So we turned Emma's camera off for that part of the conversation. Ghalib was twenty-three years old and was originally from Raqqah, a city in the Northern part of Syria. He had arrived in Amman, after having had to flee his country, about a year earlier.

He told us that he had been a soldier in the army, fighting for Bashar al-Assad. One day, he was at his post, observing the streets from the window of a building, looking through the peephole of his rifle, when he saw a man, dressed in black, suspiciously lurking around. He kept his eye on the man, already a bit unsure about his intentions. Ghalib then saw him walk up to a woman whom he knew from around the neighbourhood, and was taken aback when the man took out a knife and killed the woman, right there, while Ghalib watched through the peephole.

Ghalib's immediate reaction was to pull the trigger. He shot the man twice; he had to be bad, Ghalib thought. Later, he found out that the man was actually a soldier, and was higher up in the ranks than he was. That is how Ghalib became targeted by the army. He was no longer safe in Syria, now persecuted by the government for murder. He would have to face retaliation if he stayed in his hometown, so he decided to leave.

He went home, packed his bags, and took off. "Alone?" I asked him. "No. Me, my dog and my *Kalashnikov*" he replied. I did not know what that was, but from Manu's laugh I assumed it was some sort of weapon. Indeed a *Kalashnikov*, I later found out, is an automatic rifle, also known as AK. Ghalib walked for about forty days, until he finally made it to the Jordanian border. It was very hard for him to get into the country; by that time Jordanians were already closing entry to Syrians. Once in Amman, Ghalib roamed the streets, homeless, for over two weeks. He had no money whatsoever, knew no one in town, and could not find a job.

When Ghalib's brother and his family arrived in Jordan some time later, they were able to lend him a hand. His brother worked in construction, and managed to offer Ghalib a job. In fact, it was while doing construction work in Manu's room that Ghalib and Manu had met each other. At that time, the building needed a new doorman, for the previous one had recently been fired. Ghalib was given the position. He got paid two hundred dinars a month, minus fifty dinars, which went to cover the costs of the small room he lived in, located inside the building he cared for. He received an additional twenty-four dinars per month from UNHCR: Ghalib was a registered refugee. This made a meagre total of less than one hundred and seventy-five dinars a month. One of the things that most bothered him about his low income, he said, was not being able to go out with his friends to clubs or bars, or to treat them to a drink every now and then.

He did not make enough and wanted to find a new job, one that paid better. If only he could make some money, sufficient to find his way to a European country and leave Jordan behind. The only reason he had not left yet was because he loved hanging out with the international students that lived in the building, and especially with Manu. They spent hours sitting outside together, smoking *argileh*, and chatting in Arabic.

Every morning Ghalib woke up at seven am; that way he could sit outside for an hour, and have some time to himself. It was one of his favourite moments of the long days he mostly spent working: washing cars, carrying water, cleaning and fixing things for the owners of the building. He did not have much free time: he had to be available always, in case his bosses needed his services.

Ghalib also told us about Patricia. He had met her during her summer vacation, which she spent in Amman. She had lived in the building that Ghalib worked in. Patricia was Spanish. Though, eventually, she did learn a few words and basic expressions, Patricia did not speak Arabic, so they understood each other by means of rudimentary body language. Every day, he told us, Ghalib accompanied Patricia to the market. When she finally left, and returned to Spain, they kept in touch via their cell phones.

Ghalib was illiterate, so they mostly sent each other emoticons: a smiley face when they had a good day, a sad face when they had a bad one. They also sent each other audio files. Every morning they sent each other the same thing, the only words Patricia understood: "How are you?" to which the other replied, "Good, thank you, and you?" He had thousands of audio files just like that, all the same: "How are you?" and "Good, thank you, and you?"

I asked him whether he liked to cook. He laughed: he loved to cook! As usual, I enquired about a favourite recipe. He did not have to think much about it. Ghalib told us about his *Galaya*. It was a very special dish for him. In fact, it was the last one he ate before leaving his hometown.

After killing that man in black, and realizing the killed man was actually an official in the government army, Ghalib had hurried home. He had packed his bags and prepared to leave with his dog and his AK, knowing that he would be in danger as long as he stayed in Syria. Before setting out though, he told us, he made sure to make time for one last, delicious, home-tasting *Galaya*. He prepared it carefully, enjoyed it, and, afterwards, took off, finally commencing the long, arduous journey that would take him to Amman.

Galaya was comforting, he said. Ghalib had been kicked out of his house early on by his father, with whom he did not have a very good relationship, and had then moved in with a friend. This friend had taught him how to make *Galaya*, a dish composed of chicken, potato and tomato. It was a simple recipe, but he loved it.

I asked him if he ever made it now that he lived in Jordan, seeing as it elicited such warm feelings of comfort and safety in him. But Ghalib did not have a kitchen in the small room he inhabited, so he could not make *Galaya* anymore. On very few, special occasions, he had been able to cook *Galaya* at friends' places. Doing so, he said, made him extremely happy.

Ghalib agreed to give me the recipe for this favourite meal of his. He and Manu set to work: Ghalib explained while Manu quickly scribbled an improvised translation. You may find the result on the next page.

Ghalib's Galaya

(For 4 people)

Ingredients:

4 Medium-sized potatoes
500g of tomatoes
4 chicken thighs
Olive oil
1 big onion
3 cloves of garlic

Instructions:

Pour abundant olive oil in a big pan and set over medium heat. Cut the potatoes into small cubes and chop the tomato, onion and garlic to desired size. When the oil is very hot, add the potatoes and fry until golden. Then, add the tomato, the onion and the chopped up garlic.

Bone the chicken thighs and fry them in a separate pan, also with abundant olive oil (Ghalib likes his food with a lot of olive oil). When they are ready, set the chicken thighs aside.

After around twenty minutes, add the chicken to the big pan, with the potatoes, tomatoes and onion. Let the ingredients cook for five minutes all together, and: voilà.

It is to be eaten with Arabic bread and without cutlery.

Bayan in the kitchen: making *Yalanji*

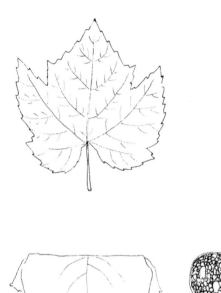

Bayan did not like to cook. Moreover, she did not like to spend time in the kitchen, but hospitable as she was she eagerly offered to teach us one of her favourite recipes just minutes after meeting us. We were introduced to Bayan at the refugee clinic during our tour around the facilities. Bayan worked for and international NGO and was filling in for a friend that day. Bayan could not answer questions about the activity the NGO carried out at the clinic, no interviews were allowed by the organization, but she said she would be more than happy to answer any general or personal questions. The result was a very informal and fun conversation.

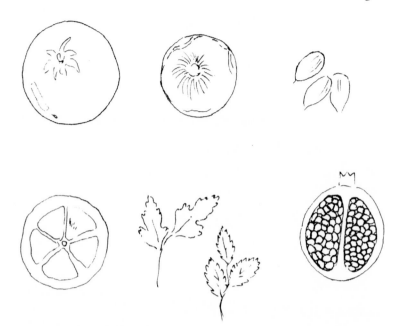

She told us she was Jordanian; she had a Jordanian passport, which is why she could legally work in Amman. But Bayan had spent most of her life, the past twenty-five of her thirty years of age, living in Syria. In many ways, she felt Syrian. Bayan had moved back to Jordan with her family a few months earlier, fleeing from the war.

When I told her about my recipe book project, she immediately invited us to her home and offered to teach us how to make stuffed grape leaves, one of her favourites, and a Syrian classic. With the help of her mother, of course, for, as she quickly informed us, Bayan did not like to cook. Later, she said, we could stay for the *Iftar* meal, break the fast with her family, and eat the results of our culinary class together. I jumped up with excitement, and gave her a huge hug, which she returned eagerly. It would be my first *Iftar* meal, I was overjoyed. We exchanged Facebook names and agreed to determine the details of our date later on. That afternoon I sent her a message asking when we could come over. "Thursday, July 2014 at 3:30 pm" she wrote back. Emma and I followed orders.

Bayan's family had a very nice apartment, somewhere quite far away: the taxi ride took forever. They were well-to-do. The house was furnished in a very Arabian way, traditional, and highly decorated. I remember a lot of embroidery, and patterns everywhere: gold and white the predominating colours. Soft carpets covered the floors.

Bayan received us in her pyjamas—consisting of colourful, matching sweat pants and a shirt—together with her adopted stray cat. Her mother was also there, a calm lady in her sixties. She was not wearing pyjamas, and she did not speak English; Bayan had to translate everything for us. The rest of the family was either working or taking an afternoon nap in an attempt to escape the hunger provoked by the long day of fasting. We would meet them later.

Emma and I were immediately scurried into the kitchen, which was already basking in wonderful smells. A pot sat bubbling on the stove, full of fragrant eggplant, slowly cooking in abundant oil. It was for the *Makhloube*, we were informed. *Makhloube* literally means upside-down and is a typical dish made of meat, vegetables and rice, which, once cooked, is served by tipping the pot upside-down onto a plate.

The grape leaves were also waiting for us there. Bayan prepared the rice and tomato stuffing, put it in a bowl and set it on a tray together with the grape leaves. Then, we all moved over to the TV room, where there were a bunch of pillows on the floor, and sat down, setting the tray in the middle. We rolled the leaves, lying on the floor, while chatting, the images of the silenced TV moving slowly in the background. It was a very soothing process. The methodical rolling was perfect for setting the appropriate mood: when you cook, the calmer you are, the better, for it is all about patience.

Once the leaves were stuffed, we went back to the kitchen and set them on the stove. Bayan's mother left to do something, so we sat down at the table and took the opportunity to really talk. Bayan did not wear a veil, though all the other female members of her family did. She had chosen not to, the same way she chose not to work in the kitchen, but to work at an international NGO instead, she told us. Bayan was not married, and she felt like others looked down on this in her community. She did not feel comfortable with the social norms prevalent in Jordan, or understood by the people around her, and wanted to move abroad. For example, though she was in her thirties, she could not stay out until later than nine when she met up with friends in the evenings.

Bayan preferred people from abroad when it came to friendships and she told us all about her many international friends, who came from all over the world, and with whom she kept in contact via Facebook, Whatsapp and the like. She had even brought an Israeli girl over to dinner once, telling her family the girl was German so as to avoid conflict: her family had Palestinian roots and would have not approved. Every day, after work, Bayan reserved two or three hours for chatting on social media with her friends. "In the end though, they always leave" she told us; their stay in the Middle East was a transient one. We would be leaving soon too.

After about an hour, the stuffed grape leaves were ready and the time for *Iftar* was approaching. Slowly the family gathered in the kitchen. Bayan's father came in, extremely elegant in his white robe and red and white Bedouin *keffuyeh*. The rest of the family lazily joined, in their pyjamas, still rubbing their eyes. We sat down and impatiently waited for the *Imam*'s signal, listening closely to the radio, and upon his prayer simultaneously broke the fast by popping a date. Dinner was scrumptious and fun, another demonstration of Middle Eastern hospitality.

We stayed for coffee, and spent another couple of hours cosily chatting in the kitchen, our bellies bursting. Bayan offered to read my future in the contents of my coffee-cup. We had been drinking Turkish coffee, which leaves a thick deposit. She turned the cup upside down on the plate and let it rest like that for a few minutes. Then, she held the cup up, very close to her face, and scrutinized it in silence, every now and then changing the angle from which she peered into it by tilting it in different directions. She then proceeded to tell me that there was a big hole in me, obviously indicated by the dark patch of coffee that stuck to one of the sides. "Very strange" she said. She also told me that I would soon run into someone from my past, someone I knew from long ago, and that we would fall in love. My future sounded o.k. So Emma asked Bayan if she would be kind enough to read hers as well. But coffee cup reading was no joke, Bayan informed us. It took up a lot of energy, and if she did it, she wanted to do it right. "Next time," she said. There was no arguing with Bayan.

By that time we had been in Bayan's house for over five hours and it was getting late. We felt it was time to leave, though we were told over and over again that it was way too early and that we could even stay over for the night if we wanted to. Indeed, they were very welcoming people. We thanked Bayan and her family for their overwhelming kindness and for the wonderful evening, and started to make our way back home with a full tummy and a plastic container holding leftover stuffed grape-leaves. At the time, we could not possibly conceive of the idea of being hungry ever again.

Bayan's Yalanji

Ingredients

A stash of dried grape leaves

For the *hashwieh*, the filling:
3 cups of white rice
4 tomatoes
1 medium onion
4 lemons
Dry mint to taste
A pinch of sugar
Olive oil to taste
Salt to taste

Instructions

Dip the grape leaves in boiling water until they soften. Leave them aside to cool.

For the *hashwieh* you will need a big bowl. Dice up the tomatoes and the onion. Add all the *hashwieh* ingredients and mix them thoroughly (the rice should be uncooked).

Take some of the broken grape leaves and cover the bottom of a big pot with a fine layer of leaves. This will prevent the stuffed leaves from burning while they cook. Set the pan aside.

Here comes the somewhat tricky, but also very fun, leaf-filling part. This part of the process takes some time, and is normally done in company. Filling and rolling grape leaves is a social experience, during which people gather and chat. You will need the soft leaves and the bowl of *hashwieh*. Take them with you and settle down somewhere comfy. This can be on the floor of your living room, in the kitchen, anywhere. Take a grape leaf and lay it out on a flat surface (if you choose to settle on the floor of the living room a large flat tray is recommended). Spread it out until it has no wrinkles. With your fingers pinch out a portion of the *hashwieh* and place it on the leaf, it should not be a big quantity for when the rice cooks it inflates and the leaf can break if there is too much stuffing. You should take just enough to make a small line of rice at the bottom of the leaf, almost touching the stem. The line should be parallel to the bottom edge of the leaf and should not reach its side edges for it will need to be folded over. Think about it like gift-wrapping, you need to leave enough space for the leaf to fold over and cover the gift: its inner content. Take the bottoms of the leaf, the protruding edges located to the right and to the left of the stem, and fold them over the rice. Then take the side edges of the leaf and fold them inwards. Now, take the bottom edge of the little package beginning to form and roll it up tightly. It is like origami. If the leaves are bigger than the palm of your hand, they are too big and need to be split in half. If you find any broken leaves, you can layer them together with other broken leaves and use them as well.

When the *hashwieh* has been used up, settle the stuffed leaves in the pot, on top of the bottom layer of leaves. Pour any left over liquid from the *hashwieh* into the pot. Add water, until the stuffed leaves are covered. You can also add more sugar and salt. Finally, pour in a bit of olive oil.

Set the pot on the stove. Leave it uncovered until it boils. For the first twenty minutes, keep the heat high, and then lower the fire until it simmers. Let the stuffed leaves cook for another thirty minutes.

Take the pot off the fire and pour out the water. Carefully set the leaves on the plate. They are ready to be eaten!

Bayan's easy-peasy fresh salad (for those who, like her, don't like to spend much time in the kitchen)

Ingredients (serves four)

3 cucumbers

3 tomatoes

1 Lemon, or lemon juice

Salt to taste

Olive oil

1 Onion

Pomegranate vinegar

Instructions

Dice up the tomatoes, cucumber and onion. Squeeze the lemon juice and mix with the salt, olive oil and pomegranate vinegar. Drizzle the mix onto the chopped vegetables. Serve as a *meze* or as an accompaniment.

Family life in Zaatari camp, and red lentil soup

One of the main focuses of our team's research was life in a refugee camp. It seemed like such a segmented experience, living in a fenced-off temporary settlement without much to do. We wanted to understand, to empathize, and to later try to communicate to others so that they too could realise what living in a refugee camp might be like.

Getting into the camps was a challenge, especially if you wanted to enter with recording materials such as cameras. Tensions within the camps were high and conflicts arose very often. The government was having a hard time ensuring security within, and wasn't too happy about journalists nosing around, but we were determined. How could we better understand the implications of the refugee status without exploring one of its most essential dimensions, that of the refugee camp? We needed media passes.

Emma was somehow able to obtain a contact within the Jordanian Government's Media Department and, after accompanying her contact to the duty free store, where he used our passports to buy all the tax-free packs of Marlboro cigarettes he could get his hands on, we finally secured four media passes into Zaatari camp.

There was, however, still one more obstacle to overcome: my mother. The Spanish embassy's webpage on travels in Jordan advised staying away from refugee camps, especially Zaatari, which was marked as a highly dangerous area. Like the Jordanian government, she was not too happy about me nosing around.

Zaatari is located a few hours' drive away from the capital, to the North of Jordan, near the Syrian border. It was built on a piece of empty, arid land. We drove up there with a local NGO, which had cars going and coming almost every day for employee transportation. Wadi came with us; he provided translating services and introduced us to refugees that we could interview who were living inside the camp. He had been there since the very beginning, actually helping set up one of the first tents, back in 2012. Wadi had witnessed Zaatari's entire evolution: he knew his way around.

We traversed miles and miles of desert-like, semi-inhabited land by car, finally making it to the big fence that outlines Zaatari's borders. There were several controls we needed to pass. Armed four-by-four vehicles, with machine guns casually set up in their back seats, surveyed the entrance, but we encountered no problems. Once inside the camp, we weren't allowed to see much or to explore, we were made to go from the car, to a secure building, and back to the car again. Our first stop was one of the many refugee clinics that had been set up by NGOs to attend the medical needs of the population, which in the beginning of September 2014 was a little under 80.000. It was early in the morning and huge lines were already developing. Many people needed medical care. The clinic's staff told us that this was partially due to the hard conditions of life in the camp.

We spent the morning walking around, as if on a guided tour, while Wadi showed us all the different departments and introduced us to the people working in each one. They were all very kind and explained to us in detail the nature of their activities. It was quite impersonal and rehearsed. They seemed so used to it: like this was part of their everyday routine. It was getting more and more uncomfortable, strolling around a refugee clinic as if it were a museum. We also stood out quite a bit: a Korean girl, a blondish European girl and two European guys. Emma and I weren't wearing Hijabs, unlike the grand majority of the women there. Our backpacks, obvious cameras and tripods did not help much either. We looked like immature journalists, in our very early twenties. I had a notebook and a pen in my hand; I wanted to record all the information that was being launched at us by the practiced staff and tried hard to ignore that taking notes made me even more of an outsider to the people visiting the clinic.

We felt extremely observed. Indeed, we were so uncomfortable that we did not dare to say a word to each other during the whole length of the clinic visit, which took about an hour. We felt the stares of the refugees, their eyes on us as we walked, and took them in in silence, wondering what they might be thinking. It seemed wrong to be a tourist of their day-to-day struggles. We knew that, and they knew that. Embarrassed, we got smaller and smaller, unconsciously shrinking away from the stares.

Finally, the tour was over, and we were able to exit the oppressive clinic. Wadi wanted to introduce us to a family he knew; they lived in a different part of the camp. We got back into the car. Once inside, the driver turned up the volume of the radio and we ended up driving around Zaatari while listening to Lady Gaga and the like, highly disturbed by the unaware nodding our heads were doing in response to the music while simultaneously witnessing the harsh conditions of the camp. Luckily the windows were shut, so outsiders were unaware of the disco sessions taking place inside the vehicle.

I peered outside the window, trying to forget the loud music. Little caravan shops lined the streets we passed, offering almost everything: not-so-fresh produce, Syrian sweets, falafels, clothes, shoes, toys, blankets, hair *scrunchies...* The camp had evolved into a little city. No one we came across during our time inside was able to explain to us how all that merchandise got into Zaatari.

Finally, the car stopped in a barer area, which only contained a few UNHCR tents and several, small, prefabricated houses. We stepped outside and knocked on the door of the nearest one.

Hadi and his family had made a cosy little home out of a caravan and a connected tent. In between the two, they had left space for a tiny patio, which was completed with a mini vegetable garden. They brought out pillows and set them on the floor, in a square. We were invited to lie down on the pillows and offered drink and food, despite the fact that it was Ramadan and the family was fasting. Of course, to show respect for the fasting, we declined the offer. We all then settled down in the shade of the patio: Hadi's family, which was made up of his parents, his two siblings and their three children, Wadi and his colleague, and us. To our surprise, the conversation quickly got animated; we had a really good time during those few hours of relaxed exchange, sitting in the shade of Wadi's improvised home.

One of the little girls, the daughter of Hadi's older sister, she must have been around seven or eight years old, took a liking to me. She fondled my earrings. I tickled the soles of her feet. Her mother explained that the girl had lost both of her earrings: one back when they were still in Raqqah, the other during their arduous journey to Jordan. At first, they would not accept the offer when I took my earrings out of my ears and handed them over to the little girl. But after a bit of insisting, she finally clenched them in her fist, with her mom's approval and a shy smile.

We asked a lot of questions with Wadi's necessary help; he translated everything. We were extremely curious about their previous and present lives. The father, we found out, was a baker. He had baked bread back in Raqqah until the cuts, which the Syrian government imposed on supplies in rebel areas, such as flour and wheat, obliged him to stop working. "No wheat: no bread". In Zaatari, he could not resume his occupation either. "All I want is to make bread again, anything to make bread," he told us. He did not enjoy the unemployed life of the refugee.

Wadi and his elder sister had been studying when the war broke out, but they couldn't continue with their studies while living in the camp. No higher education was offered there, and it was way too expensive to travel outside. "What do you do then?" We asked. They told us that daily activities mainly consisted in visiting the family next door, or the friends that lived a few tents away. Sometimes, Hadi, who was twenty-one, would even venture into surrounding villages with other youth, but that was it.

After a couple of hours of enquiring about their lives, we finally asked them if they had any questions for us. This was something we always did at the end of interviews. It was at that moment that the mother, who until then had been hiding in a corner while quietly observing, slowly leaned into the circle while looking at me, and asked: "Are you engaged?"

We all had to laugh. "No," I answered, "unfortunately not". She was very happy with my reply, she pointed at her son and with a tiny smile and a laugh she exclaimed "Hadi!"

Hadi, they told us, had a girlfriend back in Raqqah. When his family decided to leave, in order to protect him from military service recruitment, he had asked his girlfriend's family for her hand. He wanted to bring her with him to Jordan, bring her to safety. However, the family did not like the idea of their little girl growing up in a refugee camp, and refused to give them permission to marry. Hadi had to leave his girlfriend behind when he fled. He missed her, he told us, and they still talked on the phone every day. His mother was obviously heartbroken by the situation, and thought I might be a good, quick fix. Hadi didn't seem too discontent with the idea either.

Once again, I steered the conversation towards food, inspired by their tiny, aromatic vegetable garden. I asked the family whether they liked to cook. Indeed, it was one of their favourite activities. Wadi took out his smartphone and showed me a picture of an *Iftar* dinner they had prepared earlier that week. It was a proper feast, a myriad of dishes bursting with colours. Hadi's mother smiled with pride, her daughter Jada, Hadi's sister, had prepared most of the meal that we were all admiring with "aws" and "oohs".

I asked Jada whether she would be willing to teach me a recipe, something she liked to prepare there in Zaatari. She offered to explain how to make red lentil soup, a traditional Middle Eastern dish, which is easy to cook, comforting, warm and filling.

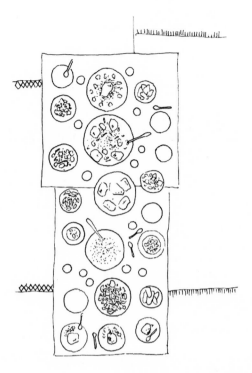

After the culinary lesson, it was time to leave. Unfortunately, the engagement fell through. It was impossible to understand each other without the help of Wadi, and we decided it would not be a practical beginning for a marriage, which would already have to overcome the problematic conditions of life in a refugee camp. An additional language barrier would just be too much. But we will always have Um Jada's *shorabet al adus,* or red lentil soup.

Um Jada's Shorabet Al Adus, or lentil soup

Ingredients

4 cups of water
150 g of onion
Ground cumin to taste
Olive oil
150 g of lentils (preferably orange or red lentils)
Salt to taste
1 cube of chicken broth

Instructions

You will need a big cooking pot. Chop the onions and fry them with a bit of oil in the big pot. Add four cups of water. Once it boils, add the lentils, a pinch of cumin, salt to taste and the cube of chicken broth. Turn the heat up. Once the mixture boils again, lower the heat and let it simmer for about an hour and fifteen minutes, or until the lentils are soft.

To enhance the taste, sprinkle the soup with lemon juice. Eat with fried pita bread.